Let's Celebrate

EARTH DAY

BY Barbara deRubertis

The Kane Press
New York

For activities and resources for this book and others in the HOLIDAYS & HEROES series, visit: www.kanepress.com/holidays-and-heroes

Acknowledgment: Our thanks to the Earth Day Network for their assistance with this book. Visit EDN online at earthday.org.

Library of Congress Cataloging-in-Publication Data

deRubertis, Barbara.
  Let's celebrate earth day / by Barbara deRubertis.
    pages cm. -- (Holidays & heroes)
  ISBN 978-1-57565-757-8 (library reinforced binding : alkaline paper) -- ISBN 978-1-57565-651-9 (paperback : alkaline paper)
  1. Environmentalism--United States--Juvenile literature. 2. Earth Day--United States--Juvenile literature. I. Title.
  GE195.5.D47 2015
  394.262--dc23
                                        2014038450
eISBN: 978-1-57565-652-6

1 2 3 4 5 6 7 8 9 10

First published in the United States of America in 2015 by Kane Press, Inc. Printed in the USA.
Book Design: Edward Miller. Photograph/Image Research: Poyee Oster.

Visit us online at **www.kanepress.com**.

 Like us on Facebook
facebook.com/kanepress

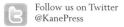 Follow us on Twitter
@KanePress

Planet Earth is a wonderful place to live! Its land and oceans are home to millions of plants and animals. The air, sunlight, water, and land provide everything needed for healthy life. And the amazing beauty of Earth fills us with awe and appreciation.

But in the 1960s, people were becoming more and more worried about the health of Planet Earth. What was causing them to worry?

In 1962, a scientist named Rachel Carson wrote a book that shocked people. *Silent Spring* was about the dangers of some of the pesticides being used on our crops to kill insects. These pesticides were also making animals and people sick.

In 1981, the United States Postal Service honored Rachel Carson with a stamp.

A pesticide called DDT caused the shells of peregrine falcon eggs to become so thin that few survived to hatch.

The air pollution in some of our big cities was also making animals and people sick. The pollution was created by burning oil, gas, and coal to run our vehicles, factories, and power plants.

Sewage and poisonous waste were being dumped into our lakes and rivers. This waste was killing fish and polluting our water supply.

Dirty water flows from a pipe polluting a river.

Oil is washed up on a beach after an oil spill.

And in 1969, there was a massive oil spill from a drilling accident off the coast of California. This spill caused many sea animals and plants to die. It damaged beaches and water. And it called for huge, costly clean-up efforts.

People said, "We have to do something to stop all this pollution!" But where to start?

A worker carefully cleans oil off of a duck after a spill.

Democratic Senator Gaylord Nelson got the idea of founding a holiday called Earth Day. He asked Republican Congressman Pete McCloskey to help him sponsor an Earth Day event on April 22, 1970. They asked a man named Denis Hayes to organize the event.

Earth Day would teach people about the environment. And people would also learn how to help solve Earth's problems.

Congressman Pete McCloskey in 1980

Senator Gaylord Nelson speaks on Earth Day, April 22, 1970.

Denis Hayes visits a dump in April 1990 and displays bottles and cans that could have been recycled instead of thrown away.

On that first Earth Day, events were held in thousands of schools and universities. Over 20 million Americans marched down streets, attended rallies, and shared ideas. They wanted laws passed that would protect the environment.

The first Earth Day, April 22, 1970. Thousands of people gathered in New York City to show their concern for the planet and all its forms of life.

The first Earth Day led to some important laws being passed by both Republicans and Democrats working together in Congress:

 The creation of the Environmental Protection Agency

 The Clean Air Act

An EPA worker tests water to make sure it's safe to drink.

The Clean Water Act

The Endangered Species Act

The laws helped limit pollution and protect our nation's air, water, land, plants, animals, and people!

Success story: Bald eagles were placed on the list of endangered and threatened species in 1967. By 2007, their numbers had increased enough for them be removed from the list.

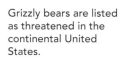

Grizzly bears are listed as threatened in the continental United States.

Green sea turtles are currently listed as endangered.

THE VOICE OF A BILLIN

From 1970 on, Earth Day has been celebrated every year on April 22, coordinated by the Earth Day Network. But when Denis Hayes began planning the 1990 Earth Day, he wanted to do something special to mark the 20th anniversary. Something BIG. So he organized a *global* Earth Day!

This time, 200 million people in 141 countries showed their support for protecting the environment. The focus of this Earth Day was the importance of *recycling*.

And ten years later, Earth Day 2000 focused on climate change and the need for clean energy. By then, environmental groups in 184 countries were reaching hundreds of millions of people.

Earth Day 2010 made "A Billion Acts of Green" its international goal for 2011. It also adopted an international plan to plant one million trees.

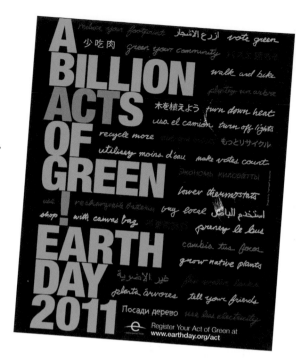

A huge crowd celebrates Earth Day 2010 at Earth Day Network's Climate Rally in Washington, D.C.

As the years pass, Earth Day focuses on new concerns and new solutions. People continue to look for the best ways to keep our planet healthy.

Today, more than a billion people around the world celebrate Earth Day on April 22.

Kids perform at an Earth Day event presented by the Earth Day Network.

But there are ways we can celebrate Earth
Day *every* day of the year. Every single day, we
can help to protect the air, water, land, plants,
animals, and people on Planet Earth!

AIR

Each time we take a breath, we use the air around us. But sometimes the air gets so dirty with pollution that it makes us sick.

What can we do? We can stop asking for unnecessary rides in gasoline-fueled cars. Every time these cars start, they add to air pollution.

Instead, we can start walking, riding bikes, or using public transportation. And we can share rides or carpool when we do need to travel in a car. In this way, we can help reduce air pollution on Planet Earth.

Kids in a carpool

WATER

In many places on Earth, there is a shortage of water. A large number of scientists think clean water is our most precious resource on Earth. But some people waste a lot of water every time they bathe, shower, or brush their teeth. This can add up to *millions* of gallons of water being wasted every year.

Women in Ethiopia carry water. In many dry countries, people must walk miles every day to bring home the water they need.

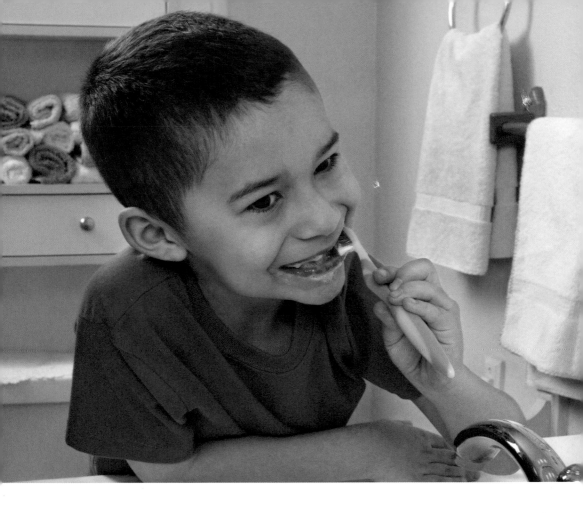

What can we do? We can use less water for baths. We can take quicker showers. And we can turn off the water while we brush our teeth.

Every time we turn off the water, we will know that we are saving a precious resource— and saving money, too!

LAND

The land on Earth fills us with wonder. High mountains. Deep canyons. Rolling hills. Flat plains.

Below the surface, the land is just as wonderful. It provides many useful resources such as oil, gas, and coal, which are often used as fuel to make energy. Much of this energy is then used for lighting, heating, and cooling our homes and schools. Appliances such as refrigerators and television sets also use energy.

The Himalayan mountains in Nepal

A large conveyor belt empties coal into an enormous pile.

But Earth's reserves of oil, gas, and coal will not last forever. These valuable resources are being used up too quickly. So it is important for people to "conserve" and use energy wisely.

What can we do? We can turn off the lights when we leave a room—even if it's just for *one minute*. We can turn on the television set only when there is a special program we want to watch. And we can put on a sweater instead of turning up the heat.

A USA "Go Green" postage stamp from 2011

PLANTS

Plants provide most of the foods we need for good health. Grains, vegetables, and fruits all come from plants. In some places, there is an abundance of food plants—but not everywhere.

There are many, many hungry people in the world—including in America. But on average, Americans throw away almost half of their food. We are feeding garbage cans and landfills instead of people!

A bulldozer enters a landfill in the mountains.

A young girl picks apples.

What can we do? We can try to be more responsible about food. First, we can choose foods that are good for us. Second, we can take *only* as much food as we need. Third, we can eat what we take.

Planet Earth is home to billions of people. And Earth Day is the one holiday we can share with all people, everywhere.

By starting with little things we can do every day, we develop Earth-wise habits. We can ask our family and friends to help. And we can join school and community efforts to pick up litter, plant trees and gardens, make posters, or hold recycling drives.

Remember: when April 22 rolls around, it's also fun to plan an Earth Day party. Do something good for the planet. Snack on healthy foods. And don't forget to wear green!

Although April 22 is the official date for Earth Day, we now know there are many, many ways to be Earth-wise every day.

A girl digs up carrots in her vegetable garden.

Remember the "gum-wrapper rule." Before
you throw a gum wrapper (or anything else) on
the ground, stop and think. What if everyone
in your school threw one gum wrapper on the
playground every day? After a few weeks, how
would your school look?

But what if everyone in your school did these little things to protect the Earth every day? What if they:

- threw away trash and recycled properly;
- rode the bus, biked, walked, or carpooled to school;
- conserved water when taking a bath or brushing their teeth;
- turned off the lights whenever they left a room; and
- tried not to waste food?

When everyone joins together to do little things, it adds up to big results.

And what if everyone, everywhere, did these same little things every day? We would see *huge* changes on Planet Earth!

Kids on a canoe trip

SAVE OUR PLANET

A girl enjoying the sun and water in Japan

A girl running in a field in Ghana

Children playing soccer in Morocco

31

Now it is our turn to take the lead in being good citizens of Planet Earth. We can practice being Earth-wise every day. We can continue to celebrate Earth Day every year. And we can learn about the best ways to solve new problems that arise.

Then we'll have a healthier Earth to pass on to *our* children. And that will be worth celebrating!

"You cannot get through a single day without having an impact on the world around you. What you do makes a difference, and you have to decide what kind of difference you want to make." —Jane Goodall